Morning Glory

Prayers, Petitions, And Purpose
In The Psalms

Jebaire Publishing, LLC
Snellville, GA

Morning Glory
Copyright©2012 Heather Arbuckle
Published by Jebaire Publishing, LLC

ISBN-13: 9780983854890

Library of Congress Control Number: 2012950761

Interior Editor: Pam Nordberg
Supervising Editor: Shannon Clark
Cover Design: Jebaire Publishing, LLC

Visit Heather Arbuckle at:
www.hearts-for-him.blogspot.com

Visit Jebaire's website at:
www.jebairepublishing.com

Dedication

Dedicated to Molly Reck and her courageous family with whom I celebrate God's amazing healing and faithfulness.

Special thanks to my extraordinary husband Marty who believed in me before I had eyes to see and to my three amazing children, Jack, Lily, and Sofie, who help me see the hope of tomorrow. I love you all to the moon and back.

Weeping may remain for a night,
but rejoicing comes in the morning.
-Psalm 30:5

Table of Contents

Prologue
Molly's Story

It is my experience that God uses the most unlikely events to serve as a catalyst for big changes in life. That is especially true when I ponder the motivation that led these devotionals to be written. For me, it all began with a prayer request. Molly Reck, a sweet girl barely three years old, was diagnosed with leukemia. Armed with nothing more than words, I sent out a prayer request for healing. Little did I know how that simple e-mail would change the direction of my life, for that awakened in me a desire to write. For the next two-and-a-half years, I wrote these devotionals for young Molly and her family as she fought bravely for her life. Molly's battle was victorious, and she now lives cancer-free. And like sweet Molly, who bravely won her battle with cancer, God's word acts as a sword in our daily battles as well. May these devotionals go out and accomplish God's purpose and bring Him glory as they ignite hope within all who read them.

Morning Glory

Prayers

Petitions

Purpose

Introduction
This is for My Glory

An ordinary day, May 29th, 2006, started like any other day. It was Friday, an end to a typical week. While I addressed the routine in my ordinary classroom, something extraordinary happened as I answered an unexpected call from my friend Gretchen Reck. Immediately, I discovered that this call was far from ordinary. In fact, this call would immediately change the course of life for a family. The sound of Gretchen's voice still haunts me, for terror had gripped my dear friend as I had never heard before. Sobbing, she had called to tell me of the doctor's suspicions . . . leukemia.

I remember that first evening, sitting in my prayer chair, lifting up hopeful cries that it was a mistake. It all felt surreal, more like a terrible nightmare than reality. I desperately hoped that any minute the phone would ring again and peace would be restored. And while I waited, my heart grieved as I pondered the unknown with fear. Nothing was as it was supposed to be, and my heart was gripped with questions for my God. "Why Molly, Lord? Why cancer? Why?" I asked boldly. And the answer was . . . "This is for My glory."

Then I received a promise that changed my heart and renewed my hope. My disillusioned eyes saw the battle before me anew from a simple promise in Psalm . . .

Weeping may remain for a night,
but rejoicing comes in the morning.
-Psalm 30:5

And as darkness crept in, God's words filled me with the peace I needed to be strong for my friend. I have never forgotten them. They have been the light in the darkness. For to me, it was a promise that Molly would be healed and that all would be well. And it was a promise that fueled every devotional written for her during her treatment. That promise has stayed with me and will endure in my heart until I step into heaven. It a promise that led me to His glory.

Sowing in Tears
Psalm 126

Have you ever stopped to consider the wonder of tears? God made us in His image, and in His creation, He placed tears. No doubt life will bring us all a fair amount of tears. Some of our tears are born of pain. With broken hearts and aching spirits, we find ourselves puzzled by circumstances beyond our control. Financial crisis. Family stress. Uncertainty and doubt. These pierce our hearts and cloud our hopes for tomorrow. And yet, as believers in Christ, we can know peace despite the mayhem all around.

It is the very assurance of our God that even when we sow in tears, we will reap a harvest of joy. And yet, we are challenged to understand the difference between the two emotions. Unlike happiness, joy is not tied to our feelings. Free from the confines of circumstance, joy is a gift we receive because of our position with God. It is an important distinction that merits mindful understanding. For, though happiness is fleeting, unbridled joy is abundant. Like rain restores the dry parched ground, our tears quench a parched spirit, renewing us and bringing us back to the One who gives life to all creation. And He promises to gather all our tears and restore us with shouts of joy, for "the LORD has done great things for us" (Psalm 126: 3).

LIFE VERSE

Those who sow in tears will reap with songs of joy!
-Psalm 126:5

Dear Heavenly Father,

We praise You for the tears You have placed in our eyes, for in our tears, we are brought ever closer to You. We praise You for You are loving and powerful, and Your eyes are always upon Your children. We thank You for the provisions You have made for us even in the midst of uncertainty. We claim the promise that even when we sow in tears, we will reap with shouts of joy. Be near to us. Draw us close. Help us to cling to You as we expectantly trust in Your timing. We love You and wait expectantly for a harvest of joy. -Amen

JOURNAL/REFLECTION

Morning Glory

This is Only a Test
Psalm 86

It is the same story every time. My stomach lurches in knots when I am faced with a test. My heart racing, I meticulously examine each question and determine the best answer with thoughtful care. When finished, I reluctantly hand in my exam, hoping for the best and feeling relieved to have it all behind me.

Life is filled with tests. We take a test to further our education. We take a test to earn a license. We even take a test to better understand our personality. With tests being such a significant part of our everyday lives, we come to feel that tests are something we have full control over. How well we do depends on how well we fix our minds on the task at hand. We determine for ourselves whether we will pass or fail. Success depends on us passing the test.

God uses tests as well. Today, let us be challenged to throw away our earthly view of tests and instead embrace God's perspective. In God's kingdom, tests are not something for which we can prepare; rather, they are used to refine and prepare us for God's eternal purpose in our lives. Often God's tests reveal themselves to us as trials. An unforeseen, often unplanned, detour changes our path and we find ourselves in unfamiliar and often unpleasant circumstances. We may be persuaded to believe we are being punished. In truth, we are being tested.

If we are to understand God's uses for testing, we must first understand what testing is NOT! First off, testing is not punishment. Our God does not punish His children; rather He disciplines us. The difference is in the definition of the two terms. Punishment involves a penalty. Discipline is loving instruction and guidance. If we meditate on God's character, we are reminded that He is "forgiving and good . . . abounding in love to all who call [on Him]" (vs. 5). It is not in God's nature to watch us squirm in His anger with punishment. Our trials are not the effect of our failure toward God. He is not surprised by any turn we take as we journey through life. However, He will allow us to be disciplined to bring us into His purpose and draw us nearer to Him.

Going further, testing is NOT temptation. The root of temptation is sin. God orders us to flee it with great haste, for sin separates us from God. However, God encourages us to endure trial and to remember "blessed is the man who perseveres under trial, because when he has stood the test, he will receive the crown of life that God has promised to those who love him" (James 1:12). Goodness and peace are the result of standing firm through Christ in trial. The tests we endure refine us and bring us into closer fellowship with God.

The entire purpose of testing is to offer revealing refinement that leads to our transformation and brings us into God's purpose. We learn much from life's tests if we trust God, remain loyal to Him, and stay committed to His plans for us. As we are tested, we learn to know God's love in new ways as we call on Him for mercy, and He answers us in faithfulness and love (vs. 6–7). Our trials sift our hearts and renew our devotion to God as we are reminded "among the gods there is none like you, O Lord; no deeds can compare with yours" (vs. 8). Our tests strengthen us and transform our character so that we may walk in truth with an undivided heart (vs. 11).

Tests are not designed to be pleasant. To the contrary, they are often quite painful. However, God does not leave us alone as we endure the trials in our midst. Instead, He offers us compassion and grace as He assures us that great is His love toward His people (vs. 13). In some way or another, we are all in the middle of a test.

Let us not overlook the confidence we have in our God. Let us persevere and be changed eternally for His glory by this test. Let us be transformed as we remember that a harvest of righteousness awaits us as we allow God to refine, strengthen, and train us for His purpose (Hebrews 12:11).

LIFE VERSE

Consider it pure joy, my brothers, whenever you face trials of many kinds, because you know that the testing of your faith develops perseverance. Perseverance must finish its work so that you may be mature and complete, not lacking anything.
-James 1:2–4

Dear Heavenly Father,

When we walk through periods of trial, we often find ourselves discouraged and confused. We may begin to believe we are being punished or tempted by You. We tire easily and become vulnerable and weak in the pain we are facing. Truly, it is more than we can endure without Your strength. Free us from the world's definition of testing and allow us to look at trials with your perspective. Let us remain joyful, for Your purpose in testing is always to bring us into Your purpose with renewed strength. We long to be transformed. Strengthen us as we endure not only this test but the trials to come. Help us to persevere in Your grace. We await Your harvest of righteousness with hearts full of longing. May You be glorified as we endure this test together. -Amen

JOURNAL/REFLECTION

A True Companion
Psalm 16

The phone rings. There is a knock at the door. Countless errands require our complete and undivided attention. The kids require a chauffeur as play dates have been scheduled and various practices require attendance. At times, the business of life makes each one of us feel as though we are the star in a Calgon commercial. We desire to be swept away from the hustle and bustle of today. No doubt, life in our technologically advanced, modern world moves pretty fast. Each busy day, distractions swirl around us with the sole purpose of silencing our ability to hear God's voice in our lives.

The world's voices distract us with noise about what we "need" in order to feel content. Distractions seem harmless enough and are revealed in innocent ways, often through the voices closest to us. But make no mistake, these voices place us in the path of deception if given the slightest bit of attention. Unfortunately, they will not be silenced with bubbles in a hot bath. If we are to ignore the distractions our enemy places near us, we must first know God's voice. All too often, these distractions appear to us as "needs."

Some distractions disguise themselves in pride. The lie we are told is that we are to keep ourselves focused on our work and prestige with a larger paycheck and an important title. We "need" to be successful in the eyes of our peers and family. As we fall into the work trap, we spend less time seeking God and more time seeking praise from our neighbors. Before we know it, we are spinning our wheels, wondering where we may find contentment or peace. Truth tells us that apart from the LORD we will have "no good thing" (vs. 2). Until we reprioritize our lives, we cannot receive the blessings that

God is ready and waiting to grant us in His perfect timing. We are challenged to let go and let God have His way in our lives, accepting His provision and assignment with humility. As we allow Him to fill our hearts with purpose, the bonds of power are broken. It is then we are free to witness the ways God will work through us to further His kingdom, rather than our bank accounts. Our egos are silenced, and we are open to the voice of the Holy Spirit.

Another common, yet dangerous distraction is materialism. Living in one of the wealthiest countries in the world, we are easily deceived about what we are entitled to. Wants soon become "needs." Houses need to be bigger, cars newer, and vacations grander as we walk through life. In time, we are enticed so much by the luxuries in our lives we no longer feel any gratitude for the comforts God has graciously placed before us.

Further, selfishness begins to grip our hearts and we grow cold in materialism. We may become so inwardly focused, we fail to hear the desperate cries of those truly in need. God's word tells us the LORD has "assigned me my portion and my cup [and He has] made my lot secure. The boundary lines have fallen for me in pleasant places [so that] I have a delightful inheritance" (vs. 5–6). God is our provider, and our blessings all come from His generous hand. In turn, a heart no longer controlled by materialism draws us nearer to God and His call on our lives.

Our enemy uses many distractions to keep us on the path of rebellion rather than obedience. Yet, you and I are secure in the promise that the LORD will remain "at my right hand [and we] will not be shaken" when we seek His counsel and instruction (vs. 8). We are called to learn His voice that rings out through the distractions in our lives. As we go to God in prayer and meditate on His word, He produces attitudes in our minds and in our hearts that will lead us on His path and help us identify the distractions.

Allow God to speak to you today and sift the distractions that threaten your contentment and your relationship with God. After all, our Father in Heaven has "made known to [us] the path of life" and fills us "with joy in [His] presence with eternal pleasures at [His] right hand" (vs. 11). Life's distractions, while enticing, simply cannot compete with our God who passionately pursues us in His love. Resolve today to no longer allow life's distractions to steal away the companionship that is yours in Christ. For, the more we know Christ, the more we will also know contentment. And contentment will silence our distractions and restore our peace.

LIFE VERSE

But my God shall supply all your need according to his riches in glory by Christ Jesus.
-Philippians 4:19 (KJV)

Dear Heavenly Father,

You are a true companion, and we come before You in humility and gratitude today. You have granted us so much and we praise You for your graciousness toward Your children. Forgive us for the way we allow the distractions in our lives to make our hearts cold to You. Be near to us and give us a renewed commitment to Your priorities. For we find true contentment and freedom as we draw nearer to You. Do not allow the distractions of this world to have any appeal to us. Rather, grant us hearts filled with Your truth, which pursues Your desires. While we do not always find comfort in our circumstances, we indeed find comfort in You. Strengthen us as we walk through our lives, and help us to embrace with humility and gratitude all You have done for us. Let us not be deceived by our enemy who wishes to draw us away from Your presence. Rather, let us be mindful that You are with us in all things. Turn our ears to Your loving voice and silence the distractions designed to fill our lives with empty deception.
-Amen

JOURNAL/REFLECTION

Know the Truth
Psalm 143

I still love the merry-go-round! As a child, I absolutely loved to spin on the merry-go-round at the school playground. With anticipation, I would hook my legs onto the bars, grip them tightly, and hang upside down as my friends and I spun faster and faster. What a thrill! When we finally came to a stop, I would stumble to the ground, stretch out flat, and watch the world spin around me as I giggled in sheer delight. It was exhilarating, and I felt so alive. As adults, we sometimes feel as though we are on that merry-go-round spinning faster and faster. Unfortunately, we don't always enjoy the ride as we did when we were younger. Truth be told, we would prefer a calmer ride where we could be still and get a grip!

The world is like a merry-go-round. It spins quickly, and we sometimes feel like we are spinning out of control along with it. Too often, I find myself weary, discouraged, or hopeless. That is not God's way. When these thoughts invade my heart, I know I have wandered away from God, and I run back to His embrace. We are walking on a rocky path as we encounter the challenges of life. The road is long and filled with peril. Our enemy would have us believe we walk it alone, but that is a lie designed to lead us out of truth. God preserves my life and yours. He silences our enemy and destroys our foes (vs. 11–12). As shield-bearers in God's army, it is important in these days that we cling to what is true about God, for perception is not reality when it comes to faith.

It is true that life is filled with challenges. However, with all the chaos that happens around us, God is in control. He does not bring us into circumstances without having an end result in mind. Every circumstance we face is allowed by God solely to bring us into His purpose. As His people, we are able to come boldly before Him in prayer and He will "hear my prayer, listen to my cry for mercy; [and in] faithfulness and righteousness come to my relief" (vs. 1–2). But we have to come to Him with an open and honest heart and be willing to let Him work. We have to give Him the control and believe He knows what is best. After all, He has walked before us, He knows the way, and He wants to carry us out of the shadows that lurk around us, into the beauty of His glory.

It is true that we have an enemy who pursues us fiercely and seeks to crush us with defeat and despair. Yet, God is faithful, and He calls us to "remember the days of long ago; . . . meditate on all [His] works and consider what [His] hands have done" (vs. 5–6). God is greater than our enemy, and He is faithful to his people. He will never let the righteous fall; rather, He holds us up when we are too weary to stand. He rescues us from our enemy and promises to work out everything for our good, despite how the circumstances appear to us in the moment. And He reassures us that we are, indeed, only in a moment. This world is not our destination. It is merely a pit stop on the way to our promised land.

No doubt, we are tempted to do things our own way. We are enticed to take our lives into our own hands and take care of the business of the day. When we act in our own strength, we quickly become weary and discouraged. God will let us go our own way, but it is not His desire. We are called to commit to God's will, regardless of the circumstances into which He calls. Our God desires for us to make Him our hiding place while He teaches us to do His will. He will preserve and restore us when we let Him work freely without interference.

God calls us to have eyes of trust. He desires for us to focus on His faithful provision, His purpose, and His constant presence rather than on the hopeless circumstances around us, which threaten our peace and lead us to exhaustion and despair. God calls us to walk in truth, and He promises to walk with us and bring us to safety.

LIFE VERSE

Blessed is the man who does not fall away on account of me.
-Luke 7:23

Dear Heavenly Father,

We praise You, for You are righteous and faithful. You have given us the Holy Spirit to lead us in truth and guide us along a straight path. You don't expect or desire for us to walk this path alone. You walk with us, encouraging us and assuring us that You know the way. Give us eyes that see Your truth despite the circumstances around us. Let us look at life with eyes of truth. Let us see You at work and have faith that this is a journey that ends in glory. Let us not be distracted by the circumstances but rather keep our eyes looking at You. Thank You for the shelter You provide in Your love, and let us not be deceived by our enemy who wishes to lure us away from Your truth.   -Amen

JOURNAL/REFLECTION

Morning Glory

Raise the White Flag
Psalm 31

My little girl is the picture of independence. Some might call it a stubborn streak. I prefer to think of it as undeveloped leadership skills waiting to take root into greatness. She takes pride in doing things for herself. Often she refuses my help, even when the task is just too big for her. Blinded by her desire to "be big," she will work herself into a frenzy while she attempts to buckle her shoes, pull her shirt over her head through the under-sized arm hole, or get her own glass of water from the bathroom sink. Only after she has exhausted all her strength will she submit to my helping hand. "Can I help you now?" I ask gently. Meekly she surrenders, crushed in self-imposed humiliation. Unfortunately, the apple doesn't fall far from the tree. All too often, I try to handle life by myself. And I would challenge that many of us are not all that different from my willful three-year-old when we find ourselves face-to-face with surrender, a powerful word rooted in the shaky foundation of pride.

Unfortunately, our worldly ideas on surrender are counterproductive in God's kingdom. When we are quite young, we are encouraged to become self-sufficient. We are trained to be brave. As we grow older, many of us mistakenly convince ourselves it is the honorable way to live. Our peers take notice and give appraisals as we describe each other as "weak" or "strong" depending on the behavior displayed before us. In our growing need for acceptance, we begin to embrace the lie of "inner strength."

In truth, we were not made to carry such a heavy burden. God never intended for us to be strong. In fact, He is most delighted when we surrender our strength and find our refuge in Him. If we simply surrender to the LORD, deliverance is ours for the taking as we remember, "You are my hiding place; you will protect me from trouble and surround me with songs of deliverance" (Psalm 32:7). God wants to be our deliverer, our protector, and our shelter. His ears are ever straining to hear us cry, "Be merciful to me, O LORD, for I am in distress; my eyes grow weak with sorrow, my soul and my body with grief. My life is consumed by anguish and my years by groaning; my strength fails because of my affliction, and my bones grow weak" (vs. 9–10). In short, He desires our surrender.

Until we lay ourselves at His feet in total submission, we will feel consumed by our need to be "strong." Submission is the complete opposite of control. It is a "voluntary yielding to another" as defined in the dictionary of my Bible. Quite simply, God seeks submission from His children. In the moment we surrender our pain, our circumstances, our trials to the LORD, we give Him permission to work in our lives and grant us peace. We should not feel shame but security in our surrender, for "our times are in [His] hands" (vs. 15). In that very moment of weakness, we can hear our Father say, "Can I help you now?" At last we are set "free . . . from the trap that is set for me, for you are my refuge" (vs. 4). Truly, it is in our complete submission that we are liberated from the confines of self-reliance. We find real strength through Christ as we surrender to God's power and sovereignty.

As the days turn to weeks and weeks to months, life passes by, and we may be tempted to believe we have been left to deal with our challenges alone. Our enemy may lead us into thinking we must put on a brave face and be strong. We may be fooled into accepting the world's view that we need to be in control. Let us remember that as we surrender and draw near to the LORD in faith, we can be assured that "the LORD preserves the faithful" (vs. 23). In His perfect timing, we will awaken to a new day of deliverance, free from the heartache of this day. Now more than ever, in our weary, weakened state, we must lift up our hands, bow our heads, and place our complete trust in our true deliverer. In our surrender, we are preserved for the deliverance of tomorrow. So let us all raise our white flags and surrender our hearts and our hurts to the LORD. And in our surrender, we can "be strong and take heart, all you who hope in the LORD" (vs. 24).

LIFE VERSE

That is why, for Christ's sake, I delight in weaknesses, in insults, in hardships, in persecutions, in difficulties. For when I am weak, then I am strong.
-2 Corinthians 12:10

Dear Heavenly Father,

We admit we often are trapped in the confines of self-reliance. We are often fooled into believing that we must be strong as we walk through heartache and trials. Deliver us from this worldly mindset, and instead fix our hearts on Your truth. Teach us to seek You in all things and to truly surrender every aspect of our lives to You. We long to be free from self-reliance. Tear down the walls that separate us from Your sovereignty, and give us hearts of submission as we take our pain to You. Let us find our strength as we take refuge in You our Deliverer. -Amen

JOURNAL/REFLECTION

The Fear Factor
Psalm 34

When I was about eight years old, I dreaded bedtime. My room was upstairs in my grandfather's old house, and each night my imagination filled with scenarios of what was potentially waiting for me in the dark enclosed staircase. Through my innocent eyes, it was a world of lurking shadows and mysterious creaks that left me feeling alone and afraid.

Each night I insisted on being escorted to the safety of my room. I would place my small hand in that of my mother, and together we would climb the stairs that seemed without end. As my heart raced, I would clutch her fingers tightly, still afraid but not alone. My mother's presence gave me the courage to stare down fear and make the journey to my warm bed in the sanctuary of my room. Once tucked in, I would find serenity in my surroundings, as my mind was now free to take notice of the provision around me. I felt the warmth of my covers take away the chill from the hard floor. My eyes would gaze upon the gentle glow in my room as the moon peeked through the window above my bed. My ears would strain to hear the gentle sounds of my mother's movements downstairs. And while I remained convinced monsters were indeed still lurking behind my curtains, my fears were put to rest. I was not alone, and I found the peace to drift off to sleep. Looking back, it is all quite amusing. And yet at the time, in my mind, my fear was real and alive.

Fortunately, I have outgrown my irrational fears of the dark, and bedtime is not such a dramatic experience for me now. I have put away childish fears of monsters in my closet. Yet, as an adult, I am at times still gripped by fear. Life happens, and sometimes I am not completely on board with the circumstances in which I find myself walking. In the midst of panic, I find myself drifting to a place of anxiety and restlessness, much like that of a child at bedtime. It happens to us all more times than we care to mention. It is in those moments that we must seek the refuge of the LORD, for He assures us that "a righteous man may have many troubles, but the LORD delivers him from them all" (vs. 19).

As our minds become distracted and our hearts fill with anxiety, we begin to feel we are walking alone. We grow afraid. Fear is our own personal internal alarm system. It indicates an absence of faith and serves as an attention-getting device. Somehow we have wandered off in doubt or self-sufficiency and find our hearts in the clutches of fear. There we are, stumbling in darkness without a night light, and the shadows and sounds surrounding us leave us feeling out of breath and immobile. We are lost in our fears. Our only escape is found in the refuge of God.

Ironically, God commands us to "Fear the LORD, you his saints, for those who fear him lack nothing" (vs. 9). However, the fear of the righteous is not based on alarm or insecurity. Rather, it is a timely surrender to the sovereignty of our LORD with reverence, adoration, and praise. When we express our devotion to God in worship, He is invited to take our hand and lead us out of fear into His perfect peace. He has walked before us, and His eyes see what ours cannot. He is aware of the sources of our fear and promises to protect us from our perceived threat. Our deliverance begins as we "extol the LORD at all times" with praise on our lips (vs. 1). As we raise our voices and seek the LORD, we are transformed. Our anxieties and restlessness drift away, and we are left with a heart prepared to hear from our Savior. We are reminded we are not alone in our troubles, for "the angel of the LORD encamps around those who fear him, and he delivers them" (vs. 7). In that moment of surrender we find solace. However, we must continue to daily seek God as "the eyes of the LORD are on the righteous and his ears are attentive to their cry"(vs. 15). Only then will we live in His perfect peace, away from fear.

As children of God, we are challenged to "seek peace and pursue it" (vs. 14). All too often life's burdens awaken fears lying dormant in many of us. Still, we are all assured that "the LORD is close to the brokenhearted" (vs. 18).

Let us lift our hands and seek out God with hearts of praise. Let us pursue Him in adoration and "exalt his name together" (vs. 3). Let us find our refuge in the One who is greater than our fear. For we can be assured that "the LORD redeems his servants; no one will be condemned who takes refuge in him" (vs. 22).

LIFE VERSE

Now fear the LORD and serve him with all faithfulness.
-Joshua 24:14

Dear Heavenly Father,

This life is filled with challenges we do not understand, and many times we are filled with anxiety and fear. With our limited perspective, we do not understand how good can possibly come out of circumstances that appear to be so out of control. We praise You, for we are never alone. Your face is upon each one of us, and You are in complete control. We thank You for the peace You promise and ask that You be our refuge in this time of healing. Let us not be distracted by the lies of fear. Bring us to deliverance as we daily seek Your presence and surrender to peace. -Amen

JOURNAL/REFLECTION

Faith vs. Feelings
Psalm 33

Driving home one evening, I felt my heart swell with love for the LORD as I sang along with the radio. While none of you would mistake my singing for actual music, I sang loud and proud anyway. As I pulled into my driveway, I was energized and rejuvenated from the exhaustion of the day. I felt utterly transformed. Often it amazes me how feelings can be so eloquently identified in song. When put to music, the highs and lows of life create memorable tunes that help us relate to one another. Music speaks to the heart from the heart. It serves as a bridge that links one life to another.

Perhaps that is why God enjoys it so much when His children "sing to him a new song; play skillfully, and shout for joy" (vs. 3). Music conveys our feelings honestly. Yet, if left unchecked, our feelings have a way of taking on a life of their own, leading us away from God's truth and into a world of dangerous illusion. In the best and worst of circumstances, we can be imprisoned in emotion as we trust our feelings without filtering them in truth. That is why God reminds us that "the word of the LORD is right and true" (vs. 4). We must not allow our feelings to control our faith. It is a road that leads to captivity.

We must use caution to monitor what we feel mirrors the truth about our Father in heaven. We must trust that "he is faithful in all he does" (vs. 4), even if our feelings blind us with confusion. We must fill our hearts with adoration and "let all the people of the world revere him" (vs. 8), especially when we feel despair. We must claim the promise that "the plans of the LORD stand firm forever" (vs. 11), even in the midst of frustration. To do otherwise is to place ourselves in the bondage of our feelings.

In truth, we cannot trust our feelings, for they are fleeting and will change momentarily with our circumstances. Instead, we must place our hope in the One who "forms the hearts of all" (vs. 15). Our God will never change, and in Him is where we are called to place our trust. When we rely on our feelings, we, in turn, place our belief in ourselves. Be advised that "no king is saved by the size of his army; no warrior escapes by his great strength" (vs. 16). If we rely on our feelings, we will be easily defeated. God has another way. God's word promises that "the eyes of the LORD are on those who fear him, on those whose hope is in his unfailing love" (vs. 18).

We cannot afford to be casual about our feelings, nor casually accept them as truth. With God's help, we can capture our feelings and send them into exile by taking spiritual inventory of our hearts. Daily, we all face a decision in battle. Either we can walk in fear and doubt, or choose to take those feelings captive. We choose between victory and victimization. In simple terms, we must capture or be captured. But we must be intentional. Today, let us choose to walk the path of faith rather than feelings. For in faith, we can "sing joyfully to the LORD . . . [as] it is fitting for the upright to praise him" (vs. 1).

LIFE VERSE

Finally, brothers, whatever is true, whatever is noble, whatever is right, whatever is pure, whatever is lovely, whatever is admirable—if anything is excellent or praiseworthy—think about such things.
-Philippians 4:8

Dear Heavenly Father,

You have given us the gift of feelings, and we thank You for the ways we are brought nearer to each other and closer to You as we share our feelings with one another. Help us to be honest with You at all times about our feelings. Remind us to take our feelings to You first, before we act out in haste because of our feelings in the moment. So often we create a prison for ourselves formed with walls created by our feelings. Tear down the walls that place us in captivity, and restore our freedom with Your truth. Place our feet upon the path of faith, and free us from the reliance we have on our feelings. Help us to, instead, rely on You. Give us intentional faith that is not weakened by the inconsistencies of our feelings. May we never forget that Your love is greater than our feelings.   -Amen

JOURNAL/REFLECTION

Got Faith?
Psalm 118

Bedtime at our house is a lengthy enterprise filled with comfort and ritual. After pajamas, books, and prayer, we turn down the covers and seek out the bedtime essentials required by our three munchkins before turning out the light. Our daughter Lily has been sleeping with her ratty blanket since her first night in this world. A gift to her from her big brother, Lily received it from him the day they met in the hospital. The blanket is tattered and faded, ripped and torn, but Lily finds comfort as she snuggles against it each night, and she absolutely refuses to sleep without it.

"I think I left my blanket downstairs," Lily whined as we finished up our bedtime routine just a few nights ago. It was a carefully disguised hint aimed directly at me and my husband. Clearly, she was hoping one of us might "volunteer" to go downstairs and get her blanket so she would not have to go herself. Tired from the day and dreading the stairs, my husband directed her to go down, grab the blanket, and to make it snappy. A baffled and confused look came over Lily's delicate face, and her big, brown eyes filled with dismay as she confessed, voice quivering, that she was afraid to walk alone. Without hesitation, my husband uttered three straightforward words. "Go with God," he said frankly.

They were concise yet powerful words which gripped my heart immediately. Since that moment, I have silently evaluated their significance. Often we face challenges that seem yielding to the outside observer and yet immobilize us in their complexities. What a privilege that we can choose to "go with God," for "in my anguish I cried to the LORD, and he answered by setting me free" (vs. 5). Regardless of our circumstances, we have a constant companion in Christ who promises that "he is my helper. I will look in triumph on my enemies" (vs. 7). God's desire is for us to reach out to the LORD in trust and allow the Holy Spirit to guide us in truth as we take refuge in Christ. Still, in moments of uncertainty, we often trade faith for doubt. Dazed by our circumstances, we begin to wonder if we can really believe God is faithful. Life has us cornered, and we perceive we are "surrounded . . . on every side" by a formidable enemy (vs. 11). Uncertain, unconfident, and unreliant upon our Savior, we wallow in a crisis of faith. Yet, in that critical moment of seeming defeat, God clutches us tightly in victory, for "I was pushed back and about to fall, but the LORD helped me. The LORD is my strength and my song; he has become my salvation" (vs. 13–14).

Each day we make a defining choice—to walk decisively in faith or to wander aimlessly in doubt. Faith requires a complete trust and reliance on God. It is a belief that God is who He promises to be, and He will do as He promises in His perfect timing. On the other hand, doubt is a cunning lie designed to rob us of the confidence we have inherited through the sacrifice of Christ. As doubt settles into our hearts, we must determine to cast it away before it is allowed to take root. Instead, we must fix our mind on truth as we recall, "The LORD's right hand has done mighty things!" (vs. 16). In remembrance we find hope, and in hope resides faith.

In the challenges to come, we will indeed be confronted by mistrust. Therefore, we must be mindful to avoid the pitfalls waiting in the shadows of doubt. We must resolve to renew our minds with faith. Relying entirely on God and walking in faith, we are assured, "Blessed is he who comes in the name of the LORD" (vs. 26). God can be trusted to lead us through the darkness of inconvenience, setbacks, and chaos. The enemy seeks to use fear to destroy our trust in God, and yet we can walk boldly in faith as we claim with certainty that "the LORD is God, and he has made his light shine upon us" (vs. 27). Despite appearances, the faithful never walk alone in their trials. Instead, we "go with God" and "his love endures forever" (vs. 29).

LIFE VERSE

*Yet he did not waver through unbelief regarding the promise of
God, but was strengthened in his faith and gave glory to
God, being fully persuaded that God had power to do
what he had promised.
-Romans 4:20–21).*

Dear Heavenly Father,

*We come to You with hearts full of praise, for You are faithful and
loving to Your people. We are amazed at Your greatness as You
deliver us from the bondage of doubt. Give us hearts filled with
faith and give us eyes of trust. Let us never doubt Your goodness
or Your great love for Your children. We thank You, for we are
in Your grasp every day through all things. May we never allow
ourselves to be deceived by doubt, but rather let us walk in faith.
-Amen*

JOURNAL/REFLECTION

Morning Glory

Seasons of Doubt
Psalm 4

Every fall, I find myself longing to run away to my parents' farm in central Iowa and enjoying a literal homegrown meal. Being a farmer's daughter, I am no stranger to the labor of reaping a harvest from tiny seeds. As a young girl, in steamy, summer heat, I spent countless summer evenings tending to my grandmother's garden. I remember a sense of anticipation as we planted the seeds in early spring. Yet my enthusiasm dramatically faded as the real work of tending to the young plants became challenging.

Gardening was, in fact, a bigger task than I ever imagined it to be. At times, I had my doubts that it was even worth the time and effort to see the task to its completion. Often it seemed so much easier to surrender the plants to the weeds and, instead, buy the vegetables at the store. My attitude changed, however, as we began to see the fruits (or vegetables) of our labor. As late summer approached and the harvest was upon us, I felt myself gripped once more with anticipation as we began to pick the peas, green beans, and tomatoes. How thrilling it was to walk into that garden and see the harvest before us! Some of my most vivid memories are of my grandmother and me shelling peas and snapping beans on lazy summer afternoons as we prepared for dinner. Sitting there together, I felt an utter sense of joy and gratitude that we had pressed on into the harvest!

Those warm evenings in the garden are often on my mind. Maybe it is because there is just nothing in this world as tasty as a homegrown Iowa tomato in late August. Yet, perhaps, it is because sowing faith into our lives is a lot like caring for the tender seedlings in my grandmother's garden. As we first step out in faith, we can easily be joyful as we "know that the LORD has set apart the godly for himself; the LORD will hear when I call to him" (vs. 3). But, eventually, we find we are gripped by the harsh labor of life, and a change takes place deep within us. In time, the weeds of doubt and discouragement creep into our minds, leaving us unsettled. We find ourselves asking, "Who can show us any good?" (vs. 6). Discouragement threatens to strangle our faith unless we press on and allow Christ to tend to our hearts with truth and thanksgiving. Our spirit is liberated from the confines of doubt as we "let the light of your face shine upon us, O LORD" (vs. 6). In our quiet moments of perseverance and honest vulnerability, our joy is richly restored.

Unfortunately, most of us mistakenly believe joy to be synonymous with happiness. While happiness is an emotion completely dependent on circumstance, joy is an attitude of gratitude. Planting seeds of faith through prayer, the faithful believe with thanksgiving and praise in all God has done, all He is doing, and all He will yet do in our lives despite our present challenges. As we praise God for His goodness, plant His word in our hearts, and invite Him to work in our lives, faith gives root to joy. However, joy cannot reside in the same heart with doubt. One of them must go.

Consider a tomato plant in a garden filled with weeds. If the plant is to thrive and produce fruit, the weeds must be pulled out by the roots. If left untended, the frail tomato plant with wilt and eventually die before we ever see the harvest. Joy is like that plant. We reap a harvest of joy in our lives when we clear our hearts of discouragement, bitterness, anger, and doubt and leave room for joy to flourish in praise and thanksgiving. Our God offers assurance that He will "give me relief from my distress; be merciful to me and hear my prayer" (vs. 1).

Roadblocks in life are merely an opportunity for God to teach His children about joy. As His people, we can take our feelings directly to our King and lay them at His feet. He takes our discouragement and casts it away as far as the east is from the west. In its place, He plants joy as we shift our focus from the weeds of discontent and press on into the harvest of faith. Today let us "lie down and sleep in peace" (vs. 8) as we allow God's seeds of joy to take root in our hearts and we anticipate the blessings of tomorrow.

LIFE VERSE

I tell you the truth, if you have faith as small as a mustard seed, you can say to this mountain, 'Move from here to there' and it will move. Nothing will be impossible for you.
-Matthew 17:20

Dear Heavenly Father,

We lift up our voices in praise and thanksgiving for Your loving care and provision for Your people. You, LORD, are with us in all things. Even in our challenges and disappointments, we are not left alone. For You are always working to bring us Your best. Though we shall know heartache, give us eyes to see Your faithfulness. Let our joy be restored daily as we choose to celebrate Your unfailing love. We are so thankful for all You have done and all that You are doing in the midst of our pain. By Your great power, we will have peace and restoration. -Amen

JOURNAL/REFLECTION

Morning Glory

Do You Feel Lucky?
Psalm 14

Luck. Chance. Karma. Coincidence. Fate. These commonly heard words have held great significance in the conversations at our home this week. One particularly relevant example occurred as my children and I were running back-to-school errands one sultry afternoon. It had been a long morning of buying shoes, standing in line, and searching for school supplies. The van was quiet as we made our way home, exhausted and ready for some quiet time. Then suddenly, to my great surprise, the silence was broken.

"I don't believe in luck," announced my nine-year-old son Jack, seemingly out of the blue. It was an intriguing start to an interesting conversation. Curious about his thoughts, I probed Jack to explain himself further. Without hesitation, Jack went on to explain that he felt it was silly that anyone would rely on luck. "After all, there is no real power in throwing salt over your shoulder or knocking on wood," he stated frankly. With confidence and certainty, he continued, "Luck is simply God working to bring you a blessing." I silently pondered the wisdom in my son's words and considered how often we get caught up in the game of chance.

Whether it is playing the lottery, wishing someone good fortune, or knocking on wood, we have all, at one time or another, given almost supernatural power to the idea of luck. As I contemplated the perspective of my son, I came to the sad conclusion that, too often, we confuse luck with blessing. Instead of giving credit to our LORD, we place our gratitude in powerless substitutes. Walking around with blinders, we forget that only "the fool says in his heart 'There is no God'" (vs. 1). We may not realize we are doing so, but frequently we reduce "blessing" to mere coincidence.

Perhaps we should meditate on what it means to receive God's blessing. According to my Bible dictionary, a blessing is defined as "divine favor, reward, or kindness." Luck has nothing to do with it. It is an intentional decision by God to grant us His best in love. We are assured that God's desire is to take His "children in His arms . . . and [bless] them" (Mark 10:16). If we take on the perspective of the world, we will be deceived into playing a helpless game of chance, leaving us filled with uncertainty, doubt, and turmoil. We must be clear about who God is and how He works if we are to truly understand God's blessing on His people and receive His peace.

Only through reflecting on God's unchanging character can we be free from the deception of chance and fully open to receiving God's blessing. For "the LORD looks down from heaven on the sons of men to see if there are any who understand, any who seek God" (vs. 2). When we look with eyes of truth, we find that God is in every detail of our lives, regardless of how big or small our circumstances appear. God promises that He "is present in the company of the righteous" (vs. 5). As God's people, we have a greater power than chance. We do not have to rely on luck. Instead, we simply need to ask and await His blessing. It is a written promise that "the LORD restores the fortunes of his people" (vs. 7). Therefore, we can be assured that our Father in heaven is aware of our needs, our desires, and our circumstances. Not only is God aware, but He is at work to bring blessing into our lives despite appearances. We may not receive our answer immediately, but God's blessing awaits us nonetheless.

We have an opportunity each day to look with eyes of faith and see our circumstances through the veil of truth. The foolish among us see this as mere "chance" or "coincidence." As God's people, we see it as nothing less than God's blessing!

Today we can resolve to never again reduce God's blessing to a simple twist of fate. Instead, let us be challenged to await God's blessing expectantly with hearts prepared to "rejoice and . . . be glad!" (vs. 7). After all, God is much too powerful to rely on luck.

He will, however, in His great love, grant us His blessing.

LIFE VERSE

And He took them up in His arms, . . . and blessed them.
-Mark 10:16 (KJV)

Dear Heavenly Father,

We praise You, God, for You are in control and at work in all things. We confess that we often reduce Your presence in our lives to sheer luck. We are ashamed that, too often, we credit chance for our many good fortunes. Too often, we look to fate instead of Your providence in meeting the challenges we face each day. Give us eyes of faith that recognize the wonder of Your blessing with gratitude and praise. Thank You for the ways You bless us each day in countless ways. You go to such great lengths to shower us in Your love. Our hearts spill over with gratitude and love for all that You have done to draw us near to You. May our voices be lifted up in praise as we rejoice in Your blessing.   -Amen

JOURNAL/REFLECTION

Scars
Psalm 44

If you look closely, you can still see the scar on my right knee. I was an impetuous little girl filled with imagination, living on a farm, and it was harvest season. Everyone was busy working, and I was bored. That fall day, I noticed a massive dual tractor tire leaning against our white picket fence. Apparently it had been left there in need of repair. I gazed upon it with eyes of wonder and envisioned myself rolling around the countryside in my own personal roller coaster. It was just sitting there like it was waiting for me, and it was just too much fun to resist! I slipped my small body in the crevice of the hard rubber tire and began to sway back and forth with all my might. I was sure I could get it rolling. I gripped the sides tightly and rested safely inside as the tire began to move. I anticipated the great adventure to come. Oh, the places I would go!

Unfortunately, the monstrosity rolled away from the fence and crashed sideways on top of my small leg, leaving a deep gash in my knee. I screamed for help, and my mother ran quickly to my aid. I remember excruciating pain as my knee swelled to the size of a grapefruit. I don't know how long it took for the bruises and the cut to heal, but in their place was left a bright red scar. Through the years, the scar has faded, but it does, in fact, still remain, as does the story of its origin.

As we walk through life, we no doubt suffer injuries. Some fade quickly. Some leave scars. All, however, tell a story. Like souvenirs of life, our scars offer remembrance. And while they tell of trial and pain, scars are also evidence of healing. Many of us choose to look upon our scars, whether emotional or physical, with disgust and remorse. Filled with a sense of regret, we wait for our scars to fade away. We hope they will simply go unnoticed. And yet, our scars are storyboards of some of life's most important lessons. As we gaze upon our scars, we remember the deliverance and rescue of our Father in heaven, who rushes to our aid in our suffering. Our scars tell of His presence, His faithfulness, and His love. But, mostly, they tell of His restoration.

Our scars tell a story of days past when we found deliverance not in our own hand but by the right hand of the LORD (vs. 3). Our scars offer an opportunity to share our battles with others as we testify of restoration through His eternal faithfulness (vs. 1–2). Our enemy would argue that we have been rejected and given "up to be devoured like sheep" (vs. 11). But our scars tell another story. For as we gaze upon them, we remember God's presence in our pain, and we claim the promise that "through you [God] we push back our enemies; through your [God's] name we trample our foes" (vs. 5). Our scars are tangible evidence of victory in Christ!

No doubt, painful seasons in life come and go, leaving us with scars. At times, painful memories of darker days seem forever burned into our hearts and minds. We long to forget, but we are scarred. Yet we must remember that while painful today, our deliverance is near. For a day is coming when trials will be behind us and we shall walk in victory. One day soon, the LORD will bind these wounds. While the scars will remain, they will tell the story of God's grace and His power. Truly, our scars will indeed bring Him glory. We will look upon these dark days, and "make our boast all day long, and we will praise your [God's] name forever" (vs. 8). It is nothing short of extraordinary that even as we were crushed and covered in darkness (vs. 19), God sent His only Son, Jesus Christ, who stretched out His arms and took on our wounds himself. By His wounds, we were brought into eternal restoration and peace with God. Indeed, we shall one day see for ourselves the scars in our Savior's nail-pierced hands, and those same scarred hands will embrace us in love. We are assured that His wounds, though deep, bring us healing. His wounds tell a story as well. It is a story of deliverance, mercy, and grace. Though life brings us pain which leaves behind its scars, our LORD will once again "rise up and help us . . . because of [His] unfailing love" (vs. 26). In turmoil, we must only call out to the One who saves. Faithfully, He comes running to our side to bear our burdens and heal our wounds.

LIFE VERSE

He himself bore our sins in his body on the tree, so that we might die to sins and live for righteousness; by his wounds you have been healed .
-1 Peter 2:24

Dear Heavenly Father,

We are so thankful for Your love and for Your gift of Jesus Christ, who died so we might know restoration with You. This life is full of trials, and we find ourselves at Your mercy. We are scarred and we are in need of Your deliverance. We give to You our broken hearts and await the day when we shall find ourselves healed and restored. May these scars bring glory to You as we continuously grow in faith and share Your story with the world. Lord, we are confident that You will raise us out of this despair, into renewed hope as we claim victory in Your precious name.   -Amen

JOURNAL/REFLECTION

Morning Glory

Come to the Banquet
Psalm 25

We all have our share of "hot buttons." You know, those petty annoyances that with the right pressure create a volatile change in our demeanor. Personally, my attitude is shaped characteristically by my appetite. I admit I tend to get a bit cranky when I am in need of a snack. On days when my temper is easily flared, those nearest and dearest to me cautiously tease that perhaps I need a cracker. Spiritual hunger works the same way. When starving for "the bread of life," one's outlook and attitude are easily swayed from hope to despair. From cheer to angst. From peace to fear. Relying on personal strength, our reserves are quickly depleted as "the troubles of my heart have multiplied" (vs. 17). Every situation that threatens your peace and has the potential to steal your joy is a carefully planned tactic in the arsenal of the enemy. Without fail, spiritual hunger is a prime contributor to our vulnerability.

Thankfully, the faithful have a far better alternative to "hunger pains" of the spirit. In trust, we are asked to bring our depleted spirits to our maker, for "the LORD confides in those who fear him; he makes his covenant known to them" (vs. 14). As life sends us challenges with busy schedules, doctor appointments, and numerous pesky demands, our spiritual reserves are quickly depleted by stress and fatigue. While in the throws of emotional bankruptcy and exhaustion, our enemy cunningly attempts to persuade us that our worst fears and anxieties are, in fact, directly upon us.

In these moments of hunger, we must choose to return to the banquet table and feast on the truth of God's word. The Spirit calls to mind that "to you, O LORD, I lift up my soul; in you I trust, O my God" (vs. 1). As we look toward heaven, we can be confident that God will indeed "guide me in your truth and teach me, for you are God my Savior, and my hope is in you all day long" (vs. 5). Despite our present challenges and life's false evidence to the contrary, "all the ways of the LORD are loving and faithful for those who keep the demands of his covenant" (vs. 10). There is no need to go hungry when His love is good and plentiful.

Daily demands no doubt bring moments of weakness and depletion. Let us feast on truth as we offer up intercessions. For a banquet awaits us all when we remember "no one whose hope is in you will ever be put to shame" (vs. 3).

LIFE VERSE

He has taken me to the banquet hall, and his banner over me is love.
-Song of Solomon 2:4

Dear Heavenly Father,

We praise You, for You are the "bread of life." How glorious it is to be one of Your precious children, basking in the glory of goodness. Truly, You are good and upright, Father. Though we come to You hungry and tired from life's responsibilities, we are also grateful to find refuge at Your table. We ask us near to You, Father, as You nourish our bodies and spirits. Thank You for the banquet of truth You have graciously placed before us as we place our hope in You, LORD.   -Amen

JOURNAL/REFLECTION

Longing and Looking
Psalm 40

Even though it was blistering hot and I feared I might indeed melt quicker than a Popsicle in July, I left the comfort provided by my overworked air-conditioner and went for my evening walk. With a heavy heart full of anxious discontent, I needed some time alone with my thoughts and with God. As I walked briskly, I was consumed with my usual worries and fears and impatiently longed for my greatest desires. Somehow, in the rhythm of my feet pounding the pavement, the melodious tunes of the birds, and the gentle hum of the locusts, my spirit began to settle down. For a moment, I was able to be still with God as I paused briefly to rest on an empty bench. My mind's focus shifted momentarily to the truth being uttered around me in God's wondrous creation. As I sat, I analyzed how the birds and the locusts were cared for though they were not aware how their needs were met, and I remembered that the same promise is given to me by my Creator. Still weary and discouraged, I thought to myself, "but I am so tired of waiting."

As I stood to make my way home, I looked into the now-glowing sky and fixed my eyes upon an airplane flying directly above me. It appeared that it was preparing for landing, and my thoughts shifted again. I pondered how the passengers were feeling on board. I wondered quietly how many were returning to Dallas permanently or were just visiting temporarily on business or pleasure. I imagined exciting reunions and loving homecomings, and my heart began to smile. I thought of others who were merely passing through on their way to some other thrilling location. Once more, a thought gently crossed my mind, "Be patient, for this is not your final destination." In that instant, I realized God had spoken to me gently and had poured His comfort into my perplexed and impatient spirit. The challenges of today are really opportunities for patience if we seize them with hope and faith. For though the final destination of any journey is exciting, it is not the only moment worth anticipating. After all, life is a continuous journey of temporary landings as we make our way home.

In truth, we are always waiting for something. Raises. Promotions. At some point in each day, we are forced to wait. It is fairly comical and ironic that we live in an era of instant coffee and fast food, and yet so much of life requires patience. With that, we are challenged whether we shall place our energy into longing or looking to the LORD. Without exception, we miss the joy of today when we place our happiness in the dreams of tomorrow. Instead, we are wise if we rest and rejoice as we wait . . . for in doing so we are honored with the opportunity to point others to Christ. After all "he put a new song in my mouth, a hymn of praise to our God. Many will see and fear and put their trust in the LORD" (vs. 3). If we look with trust and patience, we witness hidden blessings which spring up with each new day as God reveals His faithfulness toward His children. Between each sunrise and sunset are opportunities for us to recall how "he lifted me out of the slimy pit, out of the mud and mire; he set my feet on a rock and gave me a firm place to stand" (vs. 2). Further, we can share God's committed work in our lives with others for "many, O LORD my God, are the wonders you have done. The things you planned for us no one can recount to you; were I to speak and tell of them, they would be too many to declare" (vs. 5).

Though life does not always go as we plan, we are called to "seek you [and] rejoice and be glad in you" (vs. 16). We must remember that God has pulled each of us through extraordinary challenges and has blessed us with His presence and provision. Let us not become discouraged but be filled with hope as we continue to witness God's movement in our lives, for "you are my help and my deliverer" (vs. 17). In these times of longing, let us not fail to "[wait] patiently for the LORD" (vs. 1). After all, we are on a journey with God, and this is not our final destination.

LIFE VERSE

Yet the LORD longs to be gracious to you; he rises to show you compassion. For the LORD is a God of justice. Blessed are all who wait for him!
-Isaiah 30:18

Dear Heavenly Father,

We praise You and thank You and lift our hearts to You as we recall the ways You have cared for us faithfully. We thank You in advance for the complete provision that awaits us in Your perfect timing. You are never early. You are never late. And You know all our needs. Help us remember to wait patiently and to rejoice in Your care. Let us be filled with peace and joy each day, rather than discontent, worry, or fear. Lord, help us to seize this time of waiting with a faith that points others to Your goodness.
-Amen

JOURNAL/REFLECTION

In Good Hands
Psalm 145

Red in the face and steaming with anger, I packed up my bag and stomped out of our small house as the screen door slammed behind. As my young feet made their way down the winding dirt drive, I replayed the great injustice handed me by my mother. Rejecting her rules and balking at her authority, I determined that life would be easier living at Grandma's. I pressed on in a rage and made plans for a new life away from the unreasonable confines of home.

Bag in hand, I planned the route in my head. Being a strong-willed six-year-old, I was certain I knew the way. I had traveled with my mother many times before, and I had paid attention to the landmarks. Surely it could not be far. Then it happened. I came to the end of the drive and met the road. A long and empty highway in rural Iowa, it stretched out in both directions as far as my eyes could see. Worse yet, I had no idea which way to go. Suddenly, I felt my eyes begin to burn, and the rage in my heart swelled into an ache in my chest as I realized the mistake I had just made in running from home. I knew I would be lost if I took one more step, and I felt completely helpless and alone. As regret began to settle on my rebellious spirit, I sat down on the grass and began to cry, too stubborn and foolish to just turn around and go back the way I came. Just then my mother, in great love and patience, came driving toward me. Though I knew she was hurt and angry, she did not say much. She just took my hand, led me to the car, and drove me back home. And though I would not yet admit it, I was thrilled that she had come to find me. After all, I was safe in her hands, and she knew the way back home.

The road of life has many turns, and sometimes we find ourselves lost. Perhaps we are filled with pride and choose to go our own way, or maybe life hands us a detour we did not anticipate. And as we encounter the unforeseen and unknown, it is our human tendency to look with worldly eyes and see only our problem staring back at us. Unable to find our way, we find ourselves stuck in fear, anxiety, or regret.

It is in these moments we must see with eyes of faith and remember whom we serve. We are the children of the LORD most high, and "his greatness no one can fathom" (vs. 3). Fully aware of our "needs" and desires, "the LORD is gracious and compassionate, slow to anger and rich in love" (vs. 8). We are assured that "the LORD is faithful to all his promises and loving toward all he has made" (vs. 13). And since our Heavenly Father has walked before us, we need not fret, for we are secure in the promise that "the LORD is near to all who call on him . . . He fulfills the desires of those who fear him; he hears their cry and saves them" (vs. 18–19).

We are challenged to fix our eyes on our sovereign LORD as we walk life's journey before us. As we step in faith each day, let us "celebrate [God's] abundant goodness and joyfully sing of [His] righteousness" (vs. 7) as we remember "the LORD upholds all those who fall and lifts up all who bow down. You open your hand and satisfy the desires of every living thing" (vs. 14, 16). The road before us is long, but we are in His good hands.

LIFE VERSE

The LORD is good, a refuge in times of trouble. He cares for those who trust in him.
-Nahum 1:7

Dear Heavenly Father,

We come before You amazed and humbled that You, our Creator, care for us so deeply. You satisfy our every need and know our every desire. Though we do not know the road before us, we find assurance that You know the way, LORD, and we are in Your hands. Thank You for loving us so completely and so faithfully. We praise You and ask You to help us place our cares in Your capable hands.   -Amen

JOURNAL/REFLECTION

Our Dwelling Place
Psalm 91

Home Sweet Home. It is my sanctuary and the dwelling of my favorite "treasures." Closing my eyes brings visions of my favorite old chair where I sit and have coffee with Jesus each morning, fine art created by my children lovingly displayed on the refrigerator, and my favorite photos and trinkets scattered carefully in every room.

No doubt about it. There's no place like home. But, more than anything else, I treasure the people who fill the rooms of my house with love, covering my heart like a warm blanket when the world is cold and dark. Whether I have been gone five minutes or five hours, I eagerly anticipate walking through my front door. Peering through the windows on my front porch, my eyes become fixed on the glow of the lights shining in the windows.

Taking in the busy activities that fill the small rooms of my house, I imagine the conversations taking place as I adoringly study my family from afar. The images, though simple, beckon me with love. I see my son relaxing on the couch as he watches his favorite cartoons. I notice my daughters playing house and dress-up. And I see my husband skillfully and lovingly managing the activities of our home in my absence. In the silence I stand with a heart of gratitude for the many blessings found here in this place of refuge. As I push through the entry and open the door, I am greeted by squeals of delight, and it is enough to fill the most weary and discouraged heart with a smile.

And yet, above all else, it is the LORD's presence that makes our home so comforting, for He has been invited to make His dwelling place here with us. Without question, the LORD is the unseen head of our home. He witnesses every activity, knows every problem, and listens to every conversation. He shares every burden and anticipates our every need. God's presence makes this ordinary house into a sanctuary for my family and me. By the power of His spirit, we are drawn near to Him and find refuge through even the most difficult situations.

God's word tells us it is the greatest desire of our LORD and Savior that He be invited to dwell in the hearts of His people. God assures us that "because he loves me . . . I will rescue him; I will protect him, for he acknowledges my name" (vs. 14). God promises us that "if you make the Most High your dwelling . . . then no harm will befall you . . . for he will command his angels concerning you to guard you in all your ways" (vs. 9–11).

With certainty, God tells us that "he who dwells in the shelter of the Most High will rest in the shadow of the Almighty (vs. 1). With God dwelling in us, we have no need for doubt, for "he is my refuge and my fortress, my God, in whom I trust" (vs. 2). Nor should we fear, as "He will cover you with his feathers, and under his wings you will find refuge; His faithfulness will be your shield and rampart" (vs. 4).

Beyond all else, God wants to dwell in your heart. When God dwells within us, we can walk through our days with assurance, as He declares that "He will call upon me, and I will answer him; I will be with him in trouble, I will deliver him and honor him" (vs. 15). Let Him be your refuge. Let Him be your shelter. Let Him be your dwelling place.

LIFE VERSE

Moreover, I will make My dwelling among you, and My soul will not reject you.
-Leviticus 26:11 (NASB)

Dear Heavenly Father,

We are amazed that You love us so much that You made a way through Christ for us to be reconciled to You and that You would choose to make Your dwelling place in our hearts. Draw us near to You, LORD, and let us know You more. Whether we be in plenty or in want, in joy or in sorrow, let us find refuge in Your presence as we allow Your spirit to dwell in us. Lord, make Yourself at home in the hearts of Your people.   -Amen

JOURNAL/REFLECTION

A Light in the Dark
Psalm 119

Shadows in the dark. We have all been the subject of nighttime torment brought on by overactive imaginations in the dead of night. For me, it was the mysterious shadows that lurked on the walls waiting to strike when the light went out. Consumed with fear, I would hide my head under the covers and cry out to the LORD to protect me from the monsters surrounding me in the dark. Though my fears were irrational, as a child, they felt as real as the darkness around me. Not surprisingly, each of my three children have at one time or another feared the "perils" of nightfall as well. For each of them, at some point, my husband and I have chased away fears with "monster spray," nightlights, lullabies, and, most of all, scripture. And yet, as much as I can assure my children that all is well, they must choose to believe or dismiss the truth.

We, as God's children, live in a dark world, tormented by the far-reaching consequences of sin. Unlike the monsters in my childhood closet, our enemy is real, not imagined. And yet, when prone to fear, we too have in front of us an elementary, fundamental choice in our response when darkness seems to be closing in around us. We need not become paralyzed in fear but rather empowered in the light of God's truth, for there is no darkness in light. We can choose darkness or light. Lies or truth. Fear or courage. It all depends on how seriously we take the promises bestowed us in God's unfailing and living word.

As we plant scripture in our hearts, we soon come to understand an empowering truth, for "Your word is a lamp to guide my feet and a light for my path" (vs. 105). We can acknowledge our suffering and cling to the hope that the LORD will "preserve my life" as He promised (vs. 107). In praise and thanksgiving, we must draw near to our Heavenly Father, as Your word is my source of hope (vs. 114). For we are assured that the LORD will indeed "sustain me . . . and I will live" (vs. 116). In short, the teaching of Your word gives light, so even the simple can understand (vs. 130). God doesn't hide from us in our moments of trial and darkness, rather, He chooses to "direct my steps according to your word" (vs. 133). Too often, it is us doing the hiding.

Day after day, month after month, the LORD has proven faithful as "your promises have been thoroughly tested" (vs. 140). With faith-building consistency, our God has shed his grace upon His broken children, lost in sin, as we collectively and confidently cry out for help and put hope in Your word (vs. 147). And through it all, one truth remains certain—"the LORD will sustain me according to [his] promise, and I will live!" (vs. 116). Not just this day, but every day, let us rise early before the sun is up, cry out for help, and "put my hope in your word" (vs. 147). In the watches of this night and every night, let us stay awake thinking about your promises (vs. 148). For we serve a God who is greater than the darkness. And there is no darkness in the light of His love.

LIFE VERSE

But you are a chosen people, a royal priesthood, a holy nation, a people belonging to God, that you may declare the praises of him who called you out of darkness into his wonderful light.
-1 Peter 2:9

Dear Heavenly Father,

Your light is a lamp to our feet. We confess that at times we struggle to cope with our perceived darkness. Help us to fix our hearts on the truth of Your promises. Let us be keenly aware of the light of Your presence. Draw us into Your word and plant Your promis-

es deep into the hearts of Your children, that we may be children of light.   -Amen

JOURNAL/REFLECTION

Dawn is Breaking
Psalm 5

Ok, I admit, I have never been much of a morning person. I know some of you are sneering at the understated truth in that last statement. Until recently, I was much more of a sunset kind of gal, never feeling the need to rise early enough to take in the golden kiss of the sun's first light. I figured the brilliant hues witnessed at 6:00 a.m. could be even better appreciated at 6:00 p.m. All that changed, however, when my family and I went camping together on a weekend in late fall.

After a long, cold night in our overcrowded tent, my kids and I woke before sunrise. My sweet husband, Marty, was still asleep, as were the campers in the sites adjoined to ours. And since my kids were growing increasingly restless, I knew I had to come up with a way to subdue the inevitable early morning bickering and preserve the peaceful slumber of those around us. Quite spontaneously, I suggested we all go for a listening walk. As we strolled down the rocky path together, a gentle breeze caressed our cheeks and beckoned us to the edge of a small peninsula overlooking Lake Texoma. Silently, we watched the sun peek over the horizon, slowly bringing light out of darkness. And in the serenity of those still moments, I experienced God's presence in ways I never have before.

As darkness faded away and the bright morning sun began to reflect over the water, my heart felt renewed peace and joy as I was reminded of God's promise of a new beginning simply with the breaking of the day. The rising sun brings us assurance "for surely, O LORD, you bless the righteous; you surround them with your favor as with a shield" (vs. 12). The dawn brings hope as we draw near to the LORD, for "in the morning, O LORD, you hear my voice; in the morning I lay my requests before you and wait in expectation" (vs. 3). In the dark moments of this life, we have a loving ear turned our way in assurance that "those who love your name may rejoice in you" (vs. 11), for "you are not a God who takes pleasure in evil" (vs. 4). To the contrary, we serve the Loving Father, who promised to "lead me, O LORD in your righteousness [and] make straight your way before me" (vs. 8).

If you look ahead, dawn is surely breaking. The night has been long, but we can see now with eyes of hope the gentle promise of light piercing the darkness. Before long, the perils of this journey will be nothing more than shadows illuminated with the hope of full remission. Let those who have walked this journey look up in anticipation, for a new day is upon us, and dawn is breaking.

LIFE VERSE

The way of the righteous is like the first gleam of dawn, which shines ever brighter until the full light of day.
-Proverbs 4:18(NLT)

Dear Heavenly Father,

We praise You for today and for the hope we find in Your presence. We thank You in advance for the victories yet to be revealed, and we praise You for the revelations You have given us in these days of prayer and healing. We offer thanks to You, LORD, as we continue to lift our hearts each and every day of this journey. -Amen

JOURNAL/REFLECTION

Morning Glory

CPSIA information can be obtained at www.ICGtesting.com
Printed in the USA
LVOW082209281012

304773LV00001B/46/P